MW01517436

Words
from the
street

Writings from Another slice
www.anotherslice.ca

Cover and inside photos by Shauna Lynn Russell

*This volume is dedicated
to all young people
coping with survival
on the streets.*

The People's
Lovely Library
Occupy Vancouver!

words

The Wonderful City of Vancouver © 2009 by Kelsey Johnson
Another Day in Paradise © 2009 by Fraggle Rawk
The Truth (hurts) © 2009 by Fraggle Rawk
Requiem of Yesteryear © 2009 by Fraggle Rawk
Societal Breakdown © 2009 by Fraggle Rawk
To You © 2009 by Fraggle Rawk
Untitled © 2009 by Sharon Small
Wonder... © 2009 by Binkie
HomeLess © 2009 by Blaze
Homeless Memories © 2009 by Venel Clark
All Hope is Lost © 2009 by Matt Piercy
Homeless Winter © 2009 by Rob
Crystal Addicted © 2009 by Matt Piercy
Prisoner of Addiction © 2009 by Matt Piercy
Untitled © 2009 by Nicole Lena Alakhverdiants
Untitled © 2009 by Anonymous
Dream of the Beginning © 2009 by Hannah Pettinto
Right Up Until the Point We Botched the Whole Damned Thing
© 2009 by Erick Green
The Dream of Trains © 2009 by White Boy
We Have That Kind of Love © 2009 by Hannah Pettinto
Stand © 2009 by Fraggle Rawk
Hoggle © 2009 by Fraggle Rawk
Beautiful? Struggle © 2009 by Fraggle Rawk
*To the people who feel the need to make a difference in the First
Nation's community* © 2009 by Henry Wesley

photographs
All photographs © 2009 by Shauna Lynn Russell

No part of this book may be reproduced in any form or by any means,
electronic or mechanical, including photocopying and recording, or by
any information storage and retrieval system without permission in
writing from the copyright holder.

Published in Canada in 2009 by SPN Publishing
ISBN 978-0-981-2088-0-0

www.anotherslice.ca

The book you hold in your hands is the result of two years of poetry that has been submitted to Another Slice, a zine and website created out of Directions Youth Services. The purpose of the zine and website (Anotherslice.ca) is to provide street entrenched youth with a venue for self-expression and thought.

As the facilitator of Slice meetings over the past two years, I have been able to witness young people showing their creative and political sides despite living extremely difficult lives.

The fact that these words have been produced by people who sleep on concrete every night is a true testament to the strength of the people who live on Vancouver's streets.

I feel this book would be best served by the following introductory piece from an Another Slice contributor.

Enjoy.

Eliah Mills, Another Slice Facilitator.

Introduction by Kelsey Johnson

The Wonderful City of Vancouver

Everyday, you walk past us, all of us and pretend we don't exist. You think we just do this for fun or out of laziness, think we are stupid but really you're the stupid one. You don't know what life is really about. You sit in your office in the tallest high rise looking down at the city. Is that all you really know how to do is look down at everyone?

You really haven't the slightest clue as to what your city is all about. People dying, hungry, families collapsing, but lets put that aside because everything is perfect in Vancouver-according to the upper class society. There are people out there needing help, and all you can do is raise your nose and ignore, pretend it isn't happening, when it comes down to it the homeless and poor are people too, and we are ALL here for a reason, so it's up to ALL of us to try and make it better. Don't just give us a dirty look and walk away; sometimes even a friendly smile can change the world. All I am saying is we need to do something about the ignorance in Vancouver. We all mean well and we're just trying to make some coin. Just like everybody else.

Contents

Another Day in Paradise

limping slowly towards the bench
day after day
plaid pants, bloodshot eyes
step after step
bag of seed
memory after memory
arthritic wrinkled hands reach
comfort after comfort
pigeon wings dance delicately on the winds of yesterday
some sort of serene peace wisdom, truth
passerby after passerby
he is but a ghost
crooked cane with such responsibility
feeling after feeling
gentle denture smile
year after year
only known to those who see
bird after bird
sunlight days and moonlit nights
beauty is in the eye of the beholder
for they are just pigeons
he is just an old man
we are all just what we are
taking time to smell the roses
innocence redeemed
reverting back into infantile tendencies
smiling for there is nothing more to do

Fraggle Rawk

The Truth (hurts)

This one is for you
you with the starbucks 100 dollar haircut
you there, the one with mcmurder double cheeseburger
super happiness
the one on the cell phone that drives 100,000 dead iraqi
mobile
to all the girls with something to prove, mini skirt mad-
ness
on granville street
to all the pretentious hippie cats that think smoking pot
will solve the world's problems
to all you douchebags, the roxy-roofie-colada-wet-
dream-hair-gel types
the ones who listen to britney spears, lindsay lohan and
think they piss perfume
the suits with expensive ties that could feed an african
family for a year
i know you probably don't hear me
i'm not sure that i speak your language
i know you probably can't see me
money seems to make one conspicuous enough to
acknowledge.

Now please, before you spit on me, study me or sweep
me underneath your carpet that stretches on like the sea
sit on this concrete
tell me how it feels
sleep under these stars
tell me how you sleep
if we strip away the layers
that make you who you think you are
what is left for you?
if we take away your cell phone
who is talking now?
if it all were to come crashing down
who will be the one left shivering in the cold?

I've come to find myself quite comfortable under this
carpet below the poverty line
my comfort is in the knowledge of the life that i know is
real
for life isn't cocktail parties and orgy's in oil
when it all comes crashing down
i will be the one to take your hand
tell you that there is life beyond your line of credit
money can't save your soul
the truth shall set you free
but then again
you can't hear me.

Fraggle Rawk

Requiem of Yesteryear

here i sit again
mentally pacing
system overload
override the program
going in circles over and over
i still hear your name
echoed in the distance
plummeting
down
down
down
over the cliffs edge
ocean of confusion
into my brain
always the same
no matter what the change
always ends up back at this stage
level up level down
screaming to the sky
S.O.S
S.O.S
save
my
soul
the end was always the beginning with you
history repeats itself no matter the cost
be that as it may
i am not what you think i am

...*continued*

i am of the light manifest
the purity that i will achieve
you do not affect me
so sick of being the victim
i believed in you
as you believed in me

and now you say its over
over and over again
crying tears of incredulity
wishing for a brighter day
i know one day it will come
flourish like a flower in the sun
I know love is not this issue
it was all too much too fast
We took on the world and made it out alive
Fleeing from vampires and from which we dare not speak

Running from shadows
facing them head on
Our time was then
our time is now
follow separate paths
all too narrow
to make it together
one day we will meet in the light
i will have my own soul
you will have yours
together join
as one
rejoice
we have finally made it
into the land of the free.

Fraggle Rawk

Societal Breakdown

Mindless debauchery of the senseless masses
lead only by blind belief
this invisible thief
in a society where only ignorance passes
brainwashed and corrupted
goodness and light interrupted
indulge in simple pleasure for the pain
for everyone walks and talks the same
A shiny fleet of robots
once human now but a cold steel frame
heads filled with empty thoughts
when you live to consume
become this nothing and eminent doom
condemned ourselves to this
minus the Utopian bliss
today is the coldest day in hell
united the lost children shall yell
for the freedom each soul deserves
but these are only words
beware of the man with nothing to lose
too many already fall victim to the red and white blues

no more will people squander hope
revolution the only antidote
strength and courage shall prevail
break the chains from this frigid tyrannical rail
shed the shackles of oppression

dont forget to mention
the lies
and the ties
that have bound us inside

from the people we are supposed to be
enemy lines have been breached
we
are
now
free
we
can
now
see
life as it is meant to be

Fraggle Rawk

To You

you call me scum
a survivalist by nature
these streets would eat you alive
"theres no pride it that kinda life now is there son?"
"im a girl, you fucking freak"
not that they would take the time to notice

give me colt 45 or death

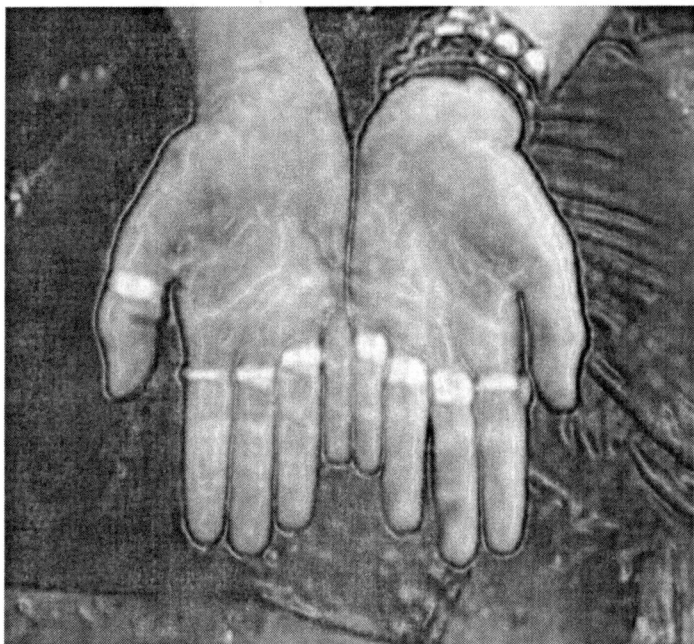

Sharon Small

Untitled

I hope you sleep well tonight
live by your own rules.
The eyes of a rich man
may call you a fool,
cause you're not spending all
your money on nice cars
and her rings.
Your not shitting out cash
cuz of the blood veins
handouts aren't free from your
family and friends
You rely on strangers
who call or pretend.

Binkie

Wonder....

I wonder why people wonder
put wondering everywhere
Guys see a really Great
looking girl I wonder how
hard it is to admire her beauty instead of offending
her by saying something rude

I wonder how and why people
wonder is it apart from the brain
why do people just Zone Out
I wonder what I could do with 1,000,000.00 I would
buy a house
and a nice bike

I wonder how someone who has
everything and lost everything
how would they survive
Yuppies suck....

Oh yea Yuppie means arrogant
SNOBB, good 4 nothing
piece of crap...

Blaze

HomeLess

Homeless that's what they call us
They say we have no homes
Because we live out on the streets
And choose to drift and roam

But, homeless is that what we truly are?
Who knows maybe it is
But what about the heroes
The women and kids

They say we choose this life of freedom
To live out on our own
To sleep beneath the stars at night
To live our lives alone

A home is just a domicide
A place to live, a house
If that's all it really is
Then I know I can live without

Some say it's where your heart is
And we hope that this is true
Cause some of us have spilt our blood
And it was red, white and blue

Some say that we are crazy
That we sold our souls too cheap
Because we'll sell our bodies
Just so our kids can eat

But if you think we choose this life
Then it's you who's lost your mind
To suggest we woke up one morning
And said I'll leave it all behind

To live the life of a prostitute,
An addict, or a drunk
To wear the same clothes everyday
That we carry in a trunk

To sell our bodies like a piece of meat
Because we cannot cope
To beg all day everyday
Just to buy the dope

To watch the people laugh at us
That look right into our face
Who forget that we are there
Unless we're in their space

...continued

Like when we beg for food
Or break into their house
To steal a million dollars
More like a sandwich or a blouse

Well now we have it,
The materialistic chain
That wraps around your human heart
Depriving oxygen to your brain

Making you think that we are homeless
Because your blind and cannot see
That a home is where your family is
And we are all your family

We might be sick and tired
We may be down and out
But we're still the long lost relatives
This world tries to forget about

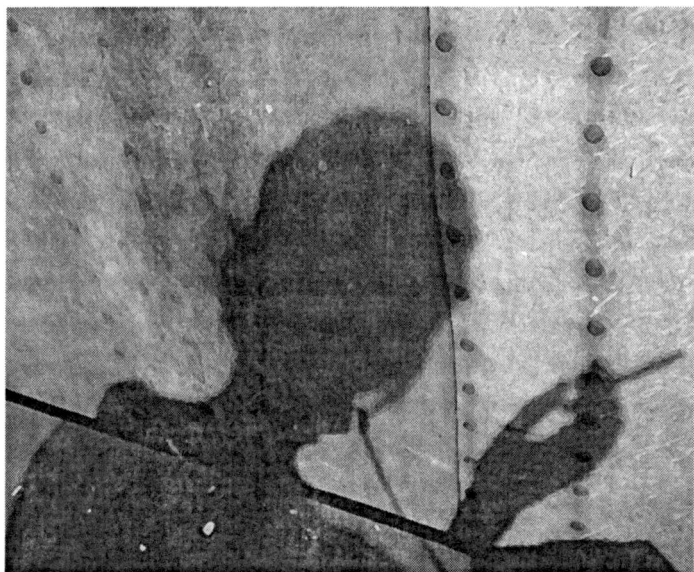

Venel Clark

Homeless memories

I was in the mist of acknowledgement, but things deprive me from accomplishment. It always occurs that I am a loser
Living in a city so connected
Keeps me farther, and closer from being a chooser. Life on the streets mind boggle me every second I don't face my own reality.
Doors keep on opening, I keep on aging
While my passion for succeeding continues relapsing.
I see rich and poor fighting for territories wanting to be memories of the next century. They scream, I talk and complain while effects of there rage tightens society free will to live to a black whole without eternity. My sainaty to a normal day is to get high and feel the burns of my misery. It hits hard on a cold day, freezing like hell, day and night the darkness in my eyes fatal to a fallen sea with no burden and prosperity. I tell myself I have fallen to a certain depth of absenity of richness, I can only hope now my god and saviour gives me forgiveness. A new life of healthy promises, that will capture my mind into a Kingdom of fallen angels. I seek that day forever and ever. It will come but pain will come first
Giving is an option + will never thirst.

...continued

You know how we say no pain no gane
Would it be the same if we were all Kings of tolerating
society where we could walk and talk the truth
without getting the booth

Its hard these days, grining and thriving in obstacles
that leads to no miracles only oracles of pain and de-
pression. It's no free ride when you have fallen from the
sky so corrupted and misunderstood it's no blue sky,
it's dark and aggravating with no good. We all want to
be on top at the speed of light, but nothing comes easy
with out a fight. Pain will all always run through the
vains of killing minds, leaving the innocent blind and
hopeless to their world of forever kings. The rich feel
some pain, the average misjudge and the poor feel rage
and hatred. The ruler of all power overtakes our sub-
conscience to feed to greed to leave us to feel so less
then shit
and spit. We all know what that is it's the value of
money that keeps biting us by the balls every time we
take a stand. Erase money we still got pain, erase pain
we got sain. If we want to continue playing what I'm
saying live day by day

not pain by money
not Joy by killing
not jealousy by stealing
Just a simple mind for living.

Matt Piercy

All Hope Is Lost

I May Seem Alright, But I'm Not Okay
Everyday Seems To Get Harder and Harder
I Must Say.
Today's Just Another Day Ending Feeling Lost
and Led Astray
I Live For Myself, A Life Lived Only For Today
I've Lost All My Faith, Lost My Urge To Pray
This Child Is Broken, And Has Lost His Way
I Can't Love Myself, Fuck If Only I Weren't Gay
Every Mid Spring, I Dread The First Of May
Why Would You Celebrate A Junkie's Birthday?
My Family Loves Me, But Their Authority I Won't Obey
All Hope Is Lost, In This Life I'm Not Meant To Stay.

Rob

Homeless Winter

So now that summer has come and left,
All our nice weather falls victim to theft.
So on with the cold rain, the winter pain
The endless days we all call lame.
We're all just looking for something to blame
But one thing's for sure, we all think the same.
My shirt is soaked and my coat full of puke,
And my dog, well, he smells my shoe,
I sit and I pan, a solution for my sorrows I ask you.
It's still raining now, soaking me through and through.
What would you say, what would you do?
Would you last a season in Vancouver Rain?
All I can do is wait it through
But time slows down when you've got nothing to do.
Have you any answers for what I have asked you?
Could you sleep in my alley while the rain blows in?
Could you tolerate the scumbags riddled with sin?
Do you know how cold it is when you have no gear?
Could you survive living in fear?
As winter sets in, so does the mood.
It turns all of us into one angry dude.
I can't wait for summer, when life out here
Is sweet as a peach.

Matt Piercy

Crystal Addicted

I look around
Feeling paranoid;
Stop fucking staring at me
Can't you leave me alone?
Hours earlier,
I kept my addiction fueled
Inhaling the vapours
Crystals creeping up my spine
The automatic feeling
Of death turning to life
The happiness and regret
Merging into a high
A sketch, a flail, if you will
I still remember,
The stupid stuff I do
And the funny pictures
That burn into my brain
We love you Trish
But don't give us lip!
Pass me the pipe
I need to flail!
Couple hours go by
Pain in your stomach spurs you on
You feel your body waste away

Grams and pounds
Drop like crazy
All from one breath of this vapour
Days go by
Sketching out for a hit of this shit
Addicted, tied down, dead inside
I can't stop because I love this
I love the pain, the concentration, the flails
Walking down Pacific Boulevard, downtown eastside
Hood up, sunglasses on
People looking for what smells
Hiding yourself away from the mistake, the relapse
The sun starts to set
And you're starting to crash
So angry
You smash the pipe, and dump the crystals
Throw away the straws and razors
Trying to remember who you are
Who loves you
Who needs you
Who you need
A few more hours go by and you're in regret
Regretting losing the drugs
Because the drugs are winning
Who are you when you're not high?

Matt Piercy

Prisoner of Addiction

High Times Are Times Held Hostage
Chemical Emotion, Synthetic Feelings
Lust Lacks Love
Rage Rampages Respect
And Hate Hijacks Happiness
Powerful indeed, the pleasurable pain we embrace is
mad.
Narcotic Gods enslave their victim like a virus
Time after Time we fall to our bloody, shattered knees
To fulfill the needs and wants of the drugs
Anything and everything we'll do it and more
Only for a point, a taste of comfortably numb
As the sand in the hourglass nears empty,
the desperation increases
The drug will succeed
And put us in the ground
The addiction put us in chains and hid us
so we'd never be found
Never to be found from our true loved ones
Until our bodies are dumped in the ground.

Anonymous

Untitled

When I was sixteen years old, I didn't care about dying. One day, I found myself in a stairwell somewhere across the bridge with no clean needles. I was young, I was stupid and I desperately needed to get high. All I had on me was a used needle that somebody had asked me to get rid of for them. As I injected myself with the used rig, HIV never even crossed my mind. The biggest regret of my life, and I can never take it back. I did the ARYS project (survey+blood test+$20) and three months later they called me in to tell me I have HIV. At that point I was so unhealthy I would have been full blown AIDS within a few months. I am so scared of dying now. The one thing I ever did in my life that put me at risk, and that was it. My last blood count was a lot better but recently my health has been getting worse again. My boyfriend doesn't have HIV and I would never forgive myself if he accidentally pricked himself with one of my needles and got it. I wish more than anything that I never used that needle. In that one moment, I feel like I have ruined my life. There is no cure for HIV, and it's been almost 5 years now. I wish that I could take it back.

I am so scared of dying now.

Anonymous

Untitled

Morning comes yet again, I can't bare the glare, of the sun, or those who'll stare. Candy for my nose, keeps me slightly composed, you'll never know the truth of my reality, and life live in, insanity.

White Devil, white devil, I am but a slave to you, I cater to you, I survive on you. I break ties for you, my secret vice, my ice. Hours I fly, eventually to crash and burn; yet again I fried my mind. No conception of time, thoughts need to stop and rewind, teeth grind, lips stained with red wine.

Shadows dance, with faces at a glance. Self inflicted addiction, a game I play with my life. The Devils dace, a destructive prance, kills all sense of anything real, I don't stand a chance. I'm messed, plagued with sleep depravation, day 5? Where am I? I shouldn't be alive, my heart shouldn't beat, what a treat, this would be, without the fight, for the right to my soul.

Tango with this devil, on his level, with his beat, I trip over my feet. Attraction, to your satisfaction, to the pleasure you give, to my alternate reality. I see the world, from a higher level, and elevated consciousness of chaotic mind fucks.

Conspiracy against me, I see, constant way to be, never to be free. At ease I'd love to be, for eternity, as Trevor chose to be. If he could see, the pain he left to me, at the hands of the devil, would it have been? Maybe he'd still breath, next to me.

I pray, for a day, just one day, to play, without you white devil. To stay awake, to not feel as though, I'm just about to break.

Sleep, precious sleep, I cant remember what your like, maybe I will when I die.

Don't cry.

Hannah Pettinto

Dream of the Beginning

These demons surround us,
The world destroys us,
We won't make it out alive,
In the deep end of death we dive,
Seeing suicide before my eyes,
Slit wrists and black tears we cry,
So deep in the vein,
"take me, I'm ready to be slain."
Death passes, and watches me suffer.
"Drag me back to hell, I'm ready to take cover."
As he watches me slowly die,
A blood puddle of sins is where I lie,
Just now realizing the pain I'm in,
Horrifying shrieks devour my soul,
Taking it, taking it somewhere cold.
Loving the feeling, making me numb,
Waiting for death, taking forever to come.

Erick Green

Right Up Until the Point We Botched The Whole Damned Thing

Tomorrow everything will be the same as it was yesterday. Today is just another two minutes on the news. That picture in your wallet, salvation, they won't bring that up. Will they? There's a million different ways to say I Love you. It's choosing the right one that's the problem. There's a million different ways to lose sight of the fact that eventually everything is comparable to a bad dream. This friendship is one. What are the others?

White Boy

The Dream of Trains

It's 2:30 in the morning. Sitting in my new North Battleford home. I just smoked a lot of good B.C. pot and fell asleep. When I wake up I'm not in inside. I'm in a train yard with trees and shrubs everywhere. As I look around I see the track with 5-48s, 3 grainners, and 4 units, with a whole bunch of other cars. I got up and packed all my shit, strapped up my pack, though it on my back. Just as I looked at the train and it started moving. Without thinking I ran, jumped on the train and crawled into a grainner. My first thought was "Where is this train going?" All I could do is wait and see. As the train pulled into the next crew change I jumped off and ran out of the yard. I saw the skytrain and knew I was in Vancouver. It was weird because I had only been on the train for an hour or so. I ran to the skytrain hopped on and... That's when I woke up.

*   *   *   *   *

*   *   *   *   *

Spiritual possession of the living we are stepping
heavily upon the beast's belly. Releasing & Reliving
Stress. Management's mission statement is a depressing
theme empty of driven purpose or worse than worthless as
an action requires no motivation just an asshole to CEO
& enough capital to veto any real flow. As for me though I
sweep the streets for IV leftovers & answer to no man that
I don't know the worth of: keeping it safe wearing the blue
gloves, Removing BioHazards for the safety of Vancity's
sons & daughters. No Track marks I thank my luck STARS

Hannah Pettinato

We have that kind of love

We have that kind of love where,
We can make joke, that is the stupidest ever, and laugh
about them for hours.
The kinda love that no matter what happens we still
make it through, good and bad.
The kinda love where we would do anything to see each
other happy, and not get mad at each other.
The kinda love where we want to spend our lives
together.
The kinda love that when we are around each other, we
forget about the world and all the drama.
The kinda love where you hold each others hands and
feel safe no matter what.
The kinda love that holding each other, makes you
happier than ever.
The kinda love that whatever song you listen to, you
can't help thinking about them.
The kinda love that you just call to say goodnight, for
their voice is the last one you would hear before you
went to bed.
The kinda love where you can sit there looking into
each others eyes, not saying a word and know
everything is going through each others heads,
The kinda love that most people want, we have.

Fraggle Rawk

Stand

he says to me i love you
like i care
like i wanted him to open his mouth and express the
unexpression, dissalusioned torment that oozes from
the wound
scattered glass
scattered brain
nsane
letting only the time float by
I saved you
letting me drown in this shallow puddle
shivering
blue lips and bloodshot eyes
reeking of cheap wisky and foul smoke
I could use a hand
I could use a hand
I could....
I would lift you out of that mire again, if only to see the
look on your face
wipe those tears from your eyes
turning the hate to love
inside
deep
deeper still
i feel the yesterdays more then i feel the tommorow

...continued

come now
for our time is short
limited time
for 6.99
plus the shipping and the gentle handling of my heart in
your hands
mold me into your little doll
it wont be long now
doc marten boots
chip toothed smile and a sideways glance
history
his story
inspiring
stringing words

stringing me along
say what you mean
mean what you dont
i know what i know and that cannot be changed
i believe in you.......
trust in me
making blind eyes see
lame legs walk
mutes talk
strip searching soul
i asked for this
confusion runs amuck
yet you stand
yet you.....
stand....

Fraggle Rawk

Hoggle

so now do you have to shake up to wake up?
such precious memories
locked into that trinket box
your inside
your outside
and everything in between
secrets promised
broken only to the token in the wind
now let it begin
empty words
leave me with an empty head
confused smile
with no alibi
wondering eyes aimed @ the sky
what will become of you?
and my
simple minded disillusionment
mistaken for a ray of sun
in this never ending rainstorm
yet i run
into what
shape or form
cookie cutter
shivering stutter
with nothing left to ponder
but my
own insecurities

now the sun has finally sunk
waiting for dawn
waiting for that light
 illuminate dark crevices
crawling with checkered letter
shady attitudes
fake emotions
cheap drinks
will my eyelashes bat @ your cheesy pick up line?
am i feeling fine?
or is it sneaking up like a creature in the shadows
roaming through acid meadows...
hand in hand
 a grain of sand
 that proverbial beach
your oh, so, crooked reach
opening locked doors into regions unknown
touchings rays of moonlight
if only in your head
even for a day
you know what I...
dont have to say
left in the yesterday that we could only imagine today
into the abyss
no longer teary eyed
walking on the left side
where else could we possibly go?
with this hitching to and fro

forsaking
condemning the risk
of never ending misinvention
without even a mention
did it really happen that fast?
take off that mask
has it really become such a task
for you
to
reveal yourself to me?
bare your soul
for i bare mine
lost the key to time
buried in the 10th detention
between the layer
of the lair
who pretends to be some one he isnt
or could never be
do you see?
can you feel the needle prick?
when did you get so sick?
general degradation
of this
non-fiction lullaby
heavy sigh
let go of my
intent
contempt
content?

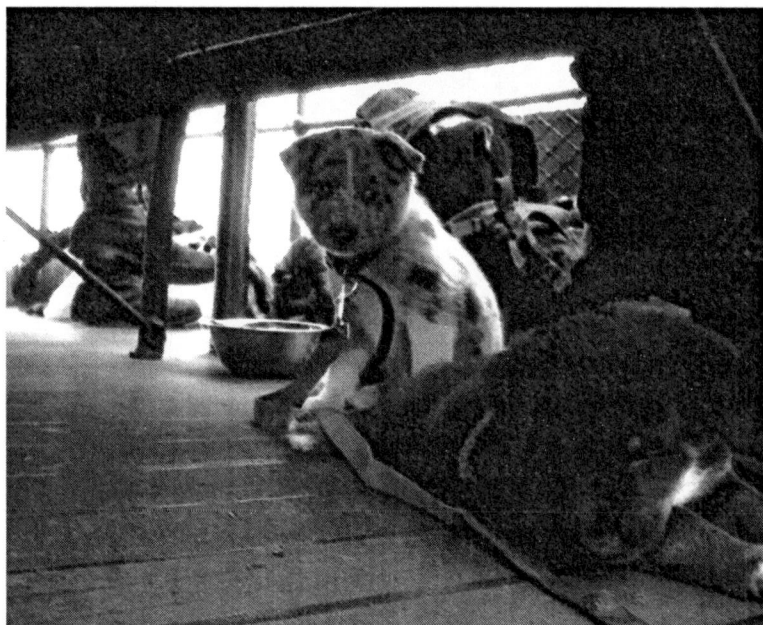

Fraggle Rawk

Beautiful? Struggle

How many words must tumble out of my mouth into my fingers and onto this paper before i feel complete?

I dont think there is a sum to the equation, then again ive never been very good at math.

KEEP YOUR CHIN UP!

So much easier said then done.

The clouds roll in again in cloud city, their menacing empty fills my head with gloomy sadness; only they can convey with such accuracy.

Have you ever seen those old ladies?

The ones with the smeared lipstick, bright red blush streaked across their cheeks trying to convey some youthful euphemisim a horrible <http://facade. no/>facade.no one is buying it. Hobbling down the street on decrepit legs too frail to support their own weight. looking to GOD, asking for some relief to the constant struggle to inhale.

this is when things fall apart...

like a 3 legged dog who is deaf in one ear and blind in one eye.

a tragic phone call

never ending

but yet dont we always pick ourselves up from this misery shrouded in mystery?

isnt that the point to our existence?

this beautiful struggle that we are faced with day after day?

we like to keep telling ourselves that

everything will be ok

do we truly believe this?

do i truly believe this??

...oh im so sorry for bringing you into my little sequence of events that have unfolded with unforseen circumstances, surely someone must have seen them coming...

i guess it just wasnt me

Henry Wesley

To the people who feel the need to make a difference in the First Nation's community

As the members of the community gathered, they all took their own oaths to represent the long family bloodline that has been passed down through the generations.

When the feast started, those who gathered on that misty rainy day stood in the garden waited for drummers to start. When it was time there were two lines of people on either sides of the plant. All people where asked to think positive thoughts and give their prayer to the creator and mother earth.

When we had picked our plants out of the ground we had to listen to the elder who was running the ceremony. Once completed, we all took our plants to the area where they will hang and dry. When this was all over we gathered to give thanks to the people who gathered and made the fresh salad straight from the garden.

When the time came john gave thanks to the quest society for donating the dear stew. This must have been very good because by the halfway point all of it was gone.

The most thanks was given to Musqueam reserve for letting the University of British Columbia start their own garden on the farm land, which of course was on the reserve.

If any thing was to be learned it was to never forget who you are as a native person and the traditional teachings that have been passed on for so many years that, guess what all you native people, I think if we keep going the same way we're going I think some day we will be world-wide as those the natives that kept teaching and just did not want to die.

Dear Reader,

This volume is supported by Family Services of Greater Vancouver and the YouthCLAIM project at the University of British Columbia.

The YouthCLAIM project, funded by the Social Sciences and Humanities Council of Canada (2006-2009), explores arts, literacy and media practices in the lives of youth.

While working with youth at the Directions zine site, we felt their work deserved quality production and a broader audience.

The work has been lightly edited as youth allowed, and is otherwise left as submitted.

Thanks to all who shared their work and lives with us during a year of Sunday evenings.

- Theresa Rogers, UBC YouthCLAIM project

Special thanks to Kari-Lynn Winters
for her creative assistance with this project.

Proceeds from the sale of this book and any donations
will go to Another Slice at the Directions Youth
Services Centre, Vancouver, Canada.

Printed in the United States
154123LV00001B/4/P